ECONOMY
OF
LOVE

Copyright 2010
by Relational Tithe, Inc.

ISBN 978-0-8341-2544-5

Printed in the United States of America

Cover and Interior Design by Arthur Cherry

10 9 8 7 6 5 4 3 2 1

ECONOMY
OF
LOVE

ACKNOWLEDGMENTS

Not unlike many other projects, *Economy of Love* is the coming together of the hard work and the working out of dreams in the lives of many wonderful people. Years ago a handful of us began to dream of what it would look like if we were to take a tithe (10%) of what we had and share 100% of it with those with whom we were in relationship. Our hearts yearned for it, but it was unlikely that any of us imagined joining forces with so many others who desired something new but old, something complex but strangely simple, something challenging but liberating. To that initial group, I'm grateful for your willingness to experiment together.

To those who are part of the current charter community of Relational Tithe and continue that experiment, to other groups that participate within Relational Tithe, and to the countless groups that continue to reimagine shared economies, your participation continues to create a reality of seamless relational redistribution and gives hope that another world is possible.

To the people who live out the stories that are retold and shared by artists such as the Work of the People, may your friendships continue to inspire the world to live differently.

Many thanks to the House Studio for sharing and spreading the vision that there is enough and that God intends for no one to be in need. The fingerprints of Isaac, Bruce, Kristen, Rachel, Scott, Travis, and Jeff are all over this project. Thanks to them for their desire to create such a tangible resource.

To my beautiful bride Meeghan, thanks for your support, involvement, reading, rereading, and writing, and for being the essence of an economy of love.

Many thanks to Shane for inspiring me and others to see that God is head over heels in love with such a beautiful and wretched world. May we lean into the experience and expression of this new life together.

Darin Petersen

INTRODUCTION

It all started with a (not at all uncommon) delay at the
Philadelphia airport. My friend Shane and I circled the
terminals in the clunky old Simple Way van, pulling off here and
there until the airport police moved us along. I can't remember
who we were picking up or if they even made it, but I clearly
remember the conversation we had as we drove in circles. We
started dreaming and scheming, "plotting goodness," as we like
to say.

We talked about all the good that could be done if the Church
were a little more organized and deliberate with our finances—
dangerous words for postmodern types like ourselves, who have
an innate distrust of systems and a suspicion of structure. But we
talked about how there is order in creation that goes all the way
back to the beginning of time—Sabbath, gleaning laws, tithing,
Jubilee; all of these were a part of the divine order of things and
were set in place by God to hold the world together.

Shane and I met several years ago at an evangelical megachurch
on the outskirts of Chicago, where we both worked as interns for
a year or so. While there we caught some great visions for how to
care for people. We also saw so clearly how far the economics

of the contemporary Church had strayed from God's economy in the early Church. As this particular church began a building expansion project costing some $50 million, our hearts broke. But it was also one of those times when we heard Jesus call us to get the log out of our own eye rather than pick the speck out of someone else's—even if it was a $50 million speck.

That's how Relational Tithe started—through the fruit of shared conversations, not just between Shane and me, but between hundreds of subversive friends all over the world. These conversations have been sparked over the past decade or so and continue today. Together we seek to be a unified community participating in the work of God in the world and in the redistribution of God's abundant kingdom.

Relational Tithe [(re)distribution] is rooted in an idea that is both new and ancient—the economy of "enough." In the economy of enough, personal enrichment takes a backseat to the needs of the community. We believe that relationship is essential to God's provision and is the ideal that must be held high in order not to slip toward the slow death of goodness under the cloak of charity. The evident lack of connection between those who have and those who don't was a primary drive for our community as we set out on this adventure together, and it remains a need that we see not only in the world outside of our community but within it as well.

Relational Tithe is a distinctive global Christian community. A group of dreamers and schemers joined together some years ago and described for themselves a reality worth living in to, inviting others to, and embodying. It is that described reality formed by Relational Tithe's founders that remains the guiding force of our expanding partnership and distinguishes the Relational Tithe community from other groups and communities seeking to do God's work in the world in their own valuable ways.

We are confident but not arrogant. We acknowledge that we are not the only way but that, if we choose to participate in this particular covenant, we believe in this specific but reforming way of participating with God and others in the work of redistributing the abundance of God's economy.

This *Economy of Love* project was initiated in friendship and, in turn, is designed to be journeyed through as a community. Though you'll notice snippets about Relational Tithe throughout (you can read more about Relational Tithe on page 110), this work is a broader story about relationship. About friendship. About caring for our neighbors with our resources. About being the hands and feet of Jesus. This is the *Economy of Love.*

Relational Tithe and this *Economy of Love* project are simply experiments to provoke the economic imagination of the Church. May it be so.

We don't want to insult anyone's intelligence, but we also realize this book has a lot of components. We hate to call this the instructions page, but some direction might be helpful.

Right?

We've laid out this book in a way that makes the most sense to us, but if another way works better for your community, go for it. We're not about boxing anyone in.

So, here goes:

This is a five-week study. Each week has its own video, and we'd recommend beginning each week with the corresponding video.

Then the book fun begins.

For some of you, you've been familiar with Relational Tithe's message for quite a while. But others may be hearing the Gospel this way for the first time. Whether you fall into one of these extremes or somewhere in the middle, we thought it

might be helpful to *see* the words from the
video—and their biblical references—rather
than just *hear* them. That's where the marked
up manuscript comes in.

Discussion questions follow. We're sure you
know what to do with those. Use as many of
them as you like.

Each chapter then has a commentary.
Why? We think it might be helpful to bring
everything into a practical context. Hopefully
you agree.

Finally, you'll find questions to consider and
ask of each other in your faith community.
They won't be easy to answer. But they
may just change your life.

Come to think of it, we hope this whole
project does that.

It's really, really difficult to understand that there is a God who is good when everything around us is so ugly and broken. And it's hard to understand that there is hope and life after death when so many people are going, "Well, is there life before death?" and "If God really loves me, then why are my kids starving to death?" And the incredible thing I think a lot of us have felt is, as we

WHY IS IT UGLY?
WHY IS IT BROKEN?
WHY DOES GOD ALLOW IT?
WHY DO I?

DO YOU KNOW
ANY OF THESE
PEOPLE?

throw those questions up at God and
we say, "God, why don"t you do something about the masses of our population that are living in poverty?" we
felt God say, "I did do something. I
made you."

And for some strange reason, God's
plan for salvation for the world is
obviously Jesus. But the wild thing
is that...maybe one of the greatest
mysteries of our faith is that as Jesus left the disciples, he said, "And

OBVIOUS? HOW?

now I am going to the Father, but
you will do the same things I"ve been
doing, and you"ll do even greater
things than these because I"m leaving
you the Spirit." That we are to continue to be God"s mystical body...that
God has no other hands but ours, no
other feet but ours. And the strange
thing is that our God does not want to
change the world without us.

‒ TANGIBLE

OUR GOD DESIRES
TO ENTER INTO
RELATIONSHIP
WITH GOD'S CREATION.

JOHN 14:12-17

CHRISTIANS (ME) AS A BARRIER TO PEOPLE MEETING JESUS?

WHOA!

Now I think that ultimately our hope is certainly that people can feel and taste the goodness of God and to find the salvation in Jesus"s love and sacrifice. Sometimes the biggest barrier to that has been Christians and has been a Church that is numb to the poverty of the world or just sees our Christianity as a ticket into heaven while ignoring the hells of the world around us. And we"re not willing to settle for that kind of Christianity. We believe in a kingdom that begins now and that the kingdom of God Jesus preached is not just something that we"re to go up to when we die but that we"re to bring down on earth as it is in heaven.

Do you agree with the statement from the video that the world is ugly and broken? How does your opinion on the state of the world shape your perspective following this statement?

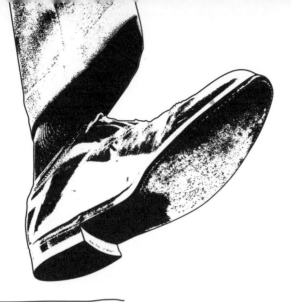

How is it possible that our sovereign, creator God "has no other hands but ours, no other feet but ours?" And what does Shane mean when he says, "The strangest thing is that our God does not want to change the world without us?"

What is Christianity
if it is more than
just a ticket into heaven?

What does it mean to bring the kingdom down to earth as it is in heaven?

The money thus collected
is deposited with the
president who takes care of
the orphans and widows
and those who are in
straits because of sickness or
any other cause and those in
prison, and visitors
from other parts.

Justin Martyr, speaking of the Sunday service in
the second century practice of the Roman church

Whoever is kind to the needy honors God.

Proverbs 14:31

On the way back from McDonald's a few days ago, I made a U-turn on 5th Street to offer my food to a stubble-faced man standing on a street corner holding a cardboard sign. I did it grudgingly to be honest, as I too often do things I believe to be good and right. The man's name is Donnie. Come to find out, he's been living under a bridge here in Columbus, Ohio, for fifteen years. He's forty years old, has no family, and told me he stopped caring about himself after his parents passed away. His great hope is to die in his sleep so he won't feel any pain.

Donnie introduced me to Trish, his friend from New Jersey. They needed a ride to the Dollar Tree so they could buy C batteries for the radio they play at night as cars pass overhead. On the way there, we listened to a hard rock radio station with the volume cranked, and when I dropped Donnie and Trish back near the bridge, they invited me to come see their house. We crossed the highway exit ramp then slid down a snow-covered hill lined with overturned grocery carts. "Sorry you have to see this," Donnie said, referring to all the trash on the ground.

Donnie and Trish live no more than two miles from
my apartment. They sleep on dirty mattresses, in
stalls separated by bridge supports. They build a fire
each night to keep warm. When I got ready to leave,
Donnie asked me to pray for them, so the three of
us joined hands, and I asked God to please take care
of my new friends, while feeling the great tension
that comes with asking to see a kingdom I know I
must help make visible. Trish prayed too. "I'm not
giving up," she told God, "not until you tell me."
Donnie said amen and I hugged them both, and
as Donnie walked me back to my car, Trish called
after me: "Don't be a stranger. Come back and see
us. We'll be here." At the top of the hill, Donnie
shook my hand and told me I'm welcome to visit
any time.

As Relational Tithe has stated elsewhere, a great tragedy of the American church is not that rich Christians do not care about the poor but that we do not *know* the poor. We who are financially secure are too often estranged from the dispossessed—insulated within our vehicles, the neighborhoods in which we choose to live, the churches we attend, the places where we shop and eat. So the poor become depersonalized, our responsibility to them often reduced to a line item in our monthly budget or to a heartfelt prayer for those in need. We speak of poverty in abstracts, not in concretes. We discuss the utility of one social program over another; we debate whether social justice is trumping other theological essentials. Important questions, these, but questions that become (if I may say so) alarmingly bourgeois when divorced from real relationship with the marginalized.

There are many days when I'd rather distance myself from those who are suffering. Meanwhile, the teachings of Scripture provoke me, and each of us, to real relationship with the Donnies and Trishes of the world, and to embrace the tension that friendships like these inevitably force upon us. This will be messy, of course. And difficult. And confusing. Truth be told, I'm not sure what my new relationships will require of me, which makes me uncomfortable. But I am called to such discomfort. We all are. And if the kingdom of God begins now, as we believe, surely it begins here—when we who make up the body of Christ resolve to create community across class lines and to test Christ's teachings with our lives.

Questions *we must ask*
One Another

What are your reactions when you see someone standing on
the side of the road holding a sign? How do you
negotiate your feelings and your response to them?
What have you learned from these encounters?

**Are you friends with anyone like Donnie or Trish?
Have you ever been Donnie or Trish?**

*In what ways are you insulated from people with physical or material
needs? How might you consistently draw nearer to such people?*

What about being in relationship with people in other socioeconomic classes makes you most anxious? What about this vision is most attractive or compelling?

Are you willing to relocate to a different neighborhood to be in relationship with less affluent people? How do you feel about this idea?

What might life before death look like for those in your city who are struggling the most?

How might you alleviate suffering in a specific way? What role can you play in making God's kingdom visible "on earth as it is in heaven?"

Exodus 5:6-21

One of the things that we see in Scripture is that God is forming a people out of the broken world that they come from. And that the story of the Exodus is the story of God rescuing a people who were slaves that were making bricks for the storehouses of Pharaoh"s economy. There was surplus, but they had no access to it.

As God leads them out of the struggle, one of the first commands that they"re given, even before the Ten Commandments, is "Do not take more than you need for each day." And that economy was one that they"re to trust that God would provide this day their daily bread.

Exodus 16:4-5; 17-19

THIS PRACTICE REMINDS US OF GOD'S ULTIMATE OWNERSHIP BY MAKING SUSTENANCE AVAILABLE TO THE POOR, THE ORPHAN, THE WIDOW, AND THE SOJOURNER.

As God is rescuing the Hebrew people from their slavery in Egypt, God begins to put some other things in place to form them as kind of God"s counterculture in the world, sort of to show the world what a society of love really looks like. And they"re to have laws like gleaning that make sure that the poor are able to have access to some of the field"s produce. They are to have special laws of how to treat the immigrant and the alien or the stranger in the land. And they are to have this beautiful celebration of the Jubilee that was to systemically dismantle the inequality of the world that we create—to make sure that land is redistributed and that slaves are set free and that debts are forgiven. All of those were ways of sort of saying, "If you don"t do these things, then you are going to end up like the empire again."

LEVITICUS 19:9-10; LEVITICUS 23:22

EXODUS 22:21; LEVITICUS 19:33-34

LEVITICUS 25:8-55

AT HARVEST, THEY WERE TO LEAVE CROPS ON THE EDGE OF THEIR LAND, AVOID GOING THROUGH THEIR FIELDS A SECOND TIME, AND LEAVE ANYTHING THAT HAD FALLEN—ALL SO THE POOR COULD TAKE THIS FOOD AND EAT.

And in the early church, there is a real sense that our rebirth has to affect our economics and how we care for our neighbor. And so John the Baptist will say "Repent, for the kingdom of God is at hand." But he will also say, "And if you've got two tunics, you need to give one away." The early Christians would say, "If we've got two coats, we've stolen one because there are still people that are cold on the street. We don't have a right to hold what's more...more for ourselves than we need while others have less than they need."

MATTHEW 3:1-2;
LUKE 3:11

And I think this idea of philanthropy or charity is actually pretty foreign to Scripture, that in the early church it was no great noble act or virtue to give to those who were poor and needy. In fact some of the early Christians would say, "When we give food to the beggar, we should get on our knees and ask for forgiveness for we are only returning what's been stolen."

God has not created one person poor
and another person rich. But we"ve
got to figure out what it really looks
like to love our neighbor as ourself.
And that"s where rebirth really de-
mands redistribution. It"s not just
a system of socialism or communism
or something like that, but it"s an
economy that is rooted in love and
real relational love for our
neighbor.

MATTHEW 22:34-40; MARK 12:28-31.

JESUS HELD OUR CARE OF EACH OTHER
IN SUCH HIGH REGARD THAT HE
NAMED THIS PRACTICE IN THE SAME
BREATH AS LOVING GOD.

ACTS 2:42-47; 4:32-37

And in the early church, one of the signs of the birthday of the early church is that they ended poverty. In Acts 2 and 4 the scripture says that "all the believers shared everything they had, and no one claimed any of their possessions were their own." And then it says, "And there were no needy persons among them." They ended poverty.

REBIRTH EXPRESSED ITSELF THROUGH REDISTRIBUTION. "NO NEEDY PERSONS AMONG THEM" IN THE FIRST CENTURY— CAN WE SAY THAT TODAY?

If you aren't sure what gleaning and
Jubilee are, take a look at the verses from
Leviticus that we noted in the video transcript.

What might these practices look like
in today's society?

How might our giving and faith
communities' budgets reflect more
fully the practices
in these scriptures?

On the video, Shane discusses believers
from both the Old and New Testaments—
and situations in which being God's people
meant
caring for the least of these.

IN WHAT WAYS ARE GOD'S PEOPLE
STILL PRACTICING THIS CARE
OF THEIR NEIGHBORS?

In what ways have we, as faith communities,
removed ourselves from these principles?

Most of us are able to feed
and house ourselves and our
families with relative ease. Keeping
basic needs such as food and
shelter in mind, consider this
sentence from the video: "There was
surplus, but they had no access to it."

How do your experiences,
economic status, and stability
color your ability to empathize
with those who have no access
to our surplus?

If it's true that
"God has not created one person poor and
another person rich,"
how do we explain the discrepancies
in our wealth? What are our
responsibilities as individuals
and faith communities to ensure
that no one goes without?

mong us English-speaking peoples especially do the praises of poverty need once more to be boldly sung. We have grown literally afraid to be poor. We despise anyone who elects to be poor in order to simplify and save his inner life. If he does not join the general scramble, we deem him spiritless and lacking in ambition. We have lost the power even of imagining what the ancient realization of poverty could have meant; the liberation from material attachments, the unbribed soul, the manlier indifference, the paying our way by what we are and not by what we have, the right to fling away our life at any moment irresponsibly—the more athletic trim, in short, the fighting shape.

William James

The LORD is my shepherd; I have all that I need.

Psalm 23:1, NLT

I just came across a black-and-white photo of Mother Teresa's old sandals—shoes so ragged and ugly and just plain uncool that if they were mine, I'd have thrown them away without a second thought. The fake leather straps have been repaired in at least two places; they look like strands of beef jerky gnawed white at the edges. The right sandal's rubber sole is worn down almost completely, and the stitching on both shoes is exposed and frayed.

All it takes is a photo and for a moment, I'm reminded that I live most days oblivious to my own wealth, comparing my standard of living to the standards of my upwardly-mobile friends and not to those of the billions of people worldwide living hand-to-mouth. And as I consider Relational Tithe's idea about enacting an economy of love, the word that seems to me to be at the heart of this different economy is the word *enough*.

For American consumerism thrives on a simple message—that what we currently have is not enough. Not big enough, not nice enough, not fast or hip enough. *Not enough* is the mantra of capitalism. At the same time, when it comes to my own economic habits, I can't simply blame the capitalist machine. Pop culture may entice me to buy things I don't need, but the truth is I like taking the bait. I like buying books instead of borrowing them from the library. I like new music and cardigan sweaters. *Not enough* is my mantra too.

But I've been thinking about the fact that the more I'm driven by an impulse to accumulate, the less free I am to meet the needs of other people—to fling away my life, as William James put it. Whether I make a lot of money or a little, the more I need—or think I need—the less I'm able to love my neighbor with my wealth. If each morning I need an Americano from my local coffee shop, I'm not necessarily greedy (or am I?); I'm just less free to feed the hungry, to clothe the naked, to live responsibly toward my fellow human beings.

Most of us are aware of this tension, and most of us care deeply about those in need. I believe that. I also believe that too often our desire to give freely of what we have gets subverted by our spending habits—by habits of consumption that seem as natural to us as walking. So part of living counterculturally, it seems to me, is being willing to consider a new standard of living—a new personal economic threshold, not oriented so much around the size of our monthly paycheck as around the value of enough.

But if I am going to really live into this economy of enough and live responsibly, it is going to take much more than living counterculturally. It will require a radical shift, a realization or remembrance that my soul is not governed by an economy developed by men of a nation, but by an economy designed by my sustainer.

Belonging to God's counterculture means placing ourselves in relationship with those who can teach us what enough really looks like. Because we can't do this alone. We need friends and guides, locally and globally, a community we can struggle with as we embrace this profoundly unfamiliar way of life. I need the help of my global family to discern when I'm consuming more than I need and causing someone else to go without. I need my decadence exposed. On the other hand, I must be reminded that if I have unmet needs, I'm part of a larger family that will help provide for me. It's through community, in other words, that we gain perspective and learn to take each other's needs seriously. We learn when to say of ourselves, *I may not have everything I want, but today, I have plenty.*

Of course, living out this value of enough will look differently for each of us. But while specifics will vary, our motive should be the same. Relational redistribution is about friendship and reminds us we are to be driven by love. Mother Teresa didn't wear beat up shoes to prove a point, after all. She wore them because she loved poor people like they were her own family. She chose simplicity not out of guilt but out of a deep reverence for all human beings.

Maybe, then, the place to start is to beg God for the kind of reverence to see our family differently and for the courage to ask difficult questions.

Questions *we must ask*
One Another

What spending habits do I need to reevaluate?
Are there any of which I need to repent?

How much is enough? How much money do I need
to keep in the bank, savings, 401k? When is my home
nice enough? My car? How many pairs of shoes
are enough? How full does my closet need to be?

How many of my possessions is it time to part with?
Which ones should go? Will I give the best ones?

What are my feelings toward people who have less than I? Do I
need to repent of certain feelings or thoughts? What are my
feelings toward people who have more than I? Do I need to repent
of certain feelings or thoughts?

Does the idea of living more responsibly, more simply, give me hope or frustrate me?

What excites or scares me about sharing my financial reality with others? When I'm asked how much money I make, what do I feel?

How does my community of faith understand greed—both individually and corporately?
How does greed disguise itself?

What does enough look like for a faith community? Do the spending patterns of our faith communities today resemble the patterns of the communities within Scripture?

LUKE 16:19-31

Jesus tells this great story of the
rich man and Lazarus. And as he tells
the parable, it"s the story of this
wealthy man who"s created a gated
neighborhood. I mean he has literally locked the poor out of his life.
And the beggar Lazarus is outside the
gate, just longing for whatever could
fall from the rich man"s table. And
the wall that he"s built between himself and the beggar becomes a wall not
just between himself and his neighbor
but between himself and God.

And the rich man, without a doubt, was a religious man. He knows the prophets, he knows the law. And yet he did not have compassion on the person right outside of his gate. And the poor man who is named in the story is Lazarus. And his name means, "The one God rescued." And when both of them come to die, the rich man, who has no name in the story…I"m sure he had a name down here (probably had a company named after him, or a town)…but he doesn"t have a name. And Lazarus, the one God rescued, is next to God.

AND THE INCREDIBLE
STORY ENDS WITH THE
RICH MAN BEGGING THE
POOR MAN FOR A DROP
OF WATER.

I think one of the things that we've found is that through our...the cultural patterns of our world that teach us to separate ourselves from the poor or from suffering, what we find out is that we end up being some of the wealthiest people in the world but also some of the most lonely and depressed and hurting people. Because what we are created for is to love and to be loved. And when we gate ourselves out, and we lock people out, and we build picket fences and gated neighborhoods and walls around our countries to lock the alien and the poor and the stranger out, we find ourselves in a place where we"re really separate from God and from those who God is so close to on the margins.

MATTHEW
22:37-40

The model of the incarnation is that Jesus moved into the neighborhood. Jesus entered into the struggle, was born in the middle of a genocide, and struggled through poverty and pain even up to the point of the cross. And that"s the model that we are called to follow.

MATTHEW 2:16-18; REMEMBER HOW, IN AN EFFORT TO ELIMINATE THE INFANT JESUS, HEROD ORDERED THE MURDER OF ALL THE BOYS IN BETHLEHEM WHO WERE TWO YEARS OLD OR UNDER?

In Luke 18:24-25, Jesus says,
"How hard it is for the rich to enter the
kingdom of God! Indeed, it is easier for
a camel to go through the eye of a needle
than for a rich man to enter the
kingdom of God."

Is this still true?

Why or why not?

Have you ever looked at a list of the wealthiest people in the world and wondered what it would be like to be one of them? Are you rich? What does it mean to be rich?

Go to globalrichlist.com to see where you fall on this list.

Jesus wasn't born
into a wealthy
family. Instead,
he was born into
a common, even
poor, family. On the
video, Shane says
that Jesus's life of
pain and poverty is
"the model that we
are called to follow."
How should our lives
reflect this model?

In Scripture we
see how God has
a special concern
for people on the
margins.

How does this
concern express
itself in
your own life?

In the life of
your congregation?

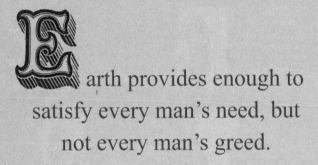

Earth provides enough to satisfy every man's need, but not every man's greed.

Mahatma Gandhi

The King will reply, "Truly I tell you, whatever you did for one of the least of these brothers and sisters of mine, you did for me."

Matthew 25:40

Even now, God desires to rescue each of us from our own brand of poverty. And we all need rescuing, especially those of us who have so embraced Western individualism that we think our goal is to have no needs we can't meet on our own—to be an island unto ourselves, self-sufficient in every practical way. The recent hurricanes and earthquakes shed light on our dilemma: in the short term, we are quick to respond with compassion to the gravest crises, when human suffering becomes most visible. In the long term though, few of us believe that we need those on the margins as much as they need us. And therein lies our peculiar brand of poverty—because we need the economically and physically vulnerable to teach us that we are also vulnerable. We need "the least of these"—the Lazaruses of the world—to help us see ourselves, and God's kingdom, differently.

This idea first came to life for me while doing relief work in Thailand following the tsunami of 2004. A fishing village had been decimated and I had joined with other aid workers to rebuild the homes of those who had survived the disaster. There was a man named Pops living in the village. He had leprosy, and he spent most days lying on a mat in the shade of a big tree near our work site, watching our progress. But on one of my last afternoons in Thailand, Pops got up from his mat, disappeared inside his small house, and emerged with a metal bowl. I watched him cradle the bowl gently with both hands as he made his way in our direction. As he came closer, I realized Pops was walking toward me, and when he got to where I was standing, he held the bowl out as if offering a gift. The bowl was filled with cold water. Pops, a leper, a man too sick to build houses, too feeble to do much of anything but lie on a mat in the shade of a tree, wanted to give me a drink.

Give a cup of cold water to one of the least of these, Jesus taught his followers, and you enter into a mysterious and profound encounter. And of all the holy moments I experienced while in Thailand, it's fair to say that this was the holiest—and the most disorienting. For in that encounter, I went from *serving* the least to *becoming* the least, and in the process I remembered something about myself I'd forgotten. I remembered that despite my economic security and relative power to affect change in the world, I'm as poor in spirit as anyone. I'm not anybody's savior; I'm just another vulnerable human being. To remember this fact was to be rescued from my own self-sufficiency and from an inflated sense of my own importance. This experience of seeing myself as one of the least was both painful and beautiful at once, which is often what it feels like to be ushered a step further into the kingdom of God.

Engaging with the world's most peripheral people is not always an easy thing to do. But listen to anyone who knows: when we live in such a way that our lives collide with the lives of the marginalized, we find we have more to receive than we have to give. We find ourselves initiated by the poor into kingdom experiences that we wouldn't have otherwise—experiences without which we would be impoverished.

So the question becomes whether we will recognize our need for those on the margins like they so often recognize their need for us. And more than that, whether we will draw near to such people—yoke our lives to theirs—to give of what we have and to receive from them in kind.

Questions *we must ask*
One Another

When you consider the Lazaruses of your neighborhood or city, who comes to mind? How do you
react to the idea that you need such people as
much as they need you?

Have you ever felt initiated into the kingdom of God by
the poor or felt that you received far more than
you gave?   Describe your experience.

Have you ever seen yourself as one of the "least of these?"
How did this experience change you?

In addition to helping us see ourselves differently,
what else do the world's most vulnerable
people have to teach us?

Are you tempted to create gates around you and your
family? How have you created gates? Has your faith
community? How can you dismantle these gates?

How do you enter relationally into the
struggles of the people in your neighborhood,
city, country, and world?

In what areas of life do you need to be
rescued from your self-sufficiency?

Your self-importance?

What will being rescued from such things require of us?

Video transcript: Shane Claiborne

MATTHEW 24:1-2;
MARK 13:1-2; LUKE 21:5-6

We"re on the steps of the Cathedral
of Saint Peter and Paul in the middle of downtown Philadelphia, and all
around us there are folks that are
homeless and hungry. In fact on rainy
days and cold nights, folks sleep on
the steps of the cathedral here. And
as we look at these buildings, I am
reminded of the story in the Gospels
where Jesus"s own disciples are mar-
veling at the architecture and the
beauty of the temple. And Jesus says
to them, "Why do you marvel at that?
One day no stone will be left on another." And it"s interesting that as
Jesus is drug before the authorities
he"s accused of subverting and trying
to destroy the temple. But Jesus just
had a new definition of what the temple
of God really is. His body. Our body.

MATTHEW 26:57-68; MARK 14:53-59

ACTS 7:48

That″s the real temple. As the book of
Acts says in the Bible, God′s Spirit
does not dwell in buildings made by
hands. But that these bodies are the
most precious thing, and the place
where we look if we want to see the
image of God.

It makes us ask though...as we think about all of the offerings that are gathered on Sunday mornings in congregations like this around the world, where is that money going? Is it still being put at the feet of the apostles and distributed to folks as they have need? It makes us wonder if in our own congregation, if there was a need or a crisis that someone had, would they know how to bring the need before the group so that people can carry the weight of that burden with them?

ARE YOUR COMMUNITY'S POOR BEING CARED FOR BY YOUR CONGREGATION?

And unfortunately the statistics and studies show over and over that very little of our church offerings are going to meet the needs of the poor among us. And much of the money that we gather on Sunday mornings is going to pay staff and build buildings, and very little of it is really going to meet the needs of the poor.

A close look at the Scriptures and the patterns from the early church reveals how the tithe was used to care for those on the margins.

Do you imitate these patterns?

Does your congregation?

Do you know where your tithe goes?

Even if your church's leadership changed nothing about how (money) is distributed, how could you, individually and as a community, still enter into relationship with and

make a difference in the lives of the marginalized in your midst?

Throughout the Bible, we see Jesus constantly surrounded by the poor and those on the margins.

How does your congregation currently care for the poor in your neighborhood—and the poor who sit next to you on Sunday?

Are you, as an individual and a congregation, in friendship with those on the margins?

Have you ever personally felt like you're one of those on the margins?

Imagine your church building
was destroyed and you could no
longer attend church services.

*Would those around you still know
you were a Christian?*

How?

 person cannot be religious
and indifferent to other
human beings' plight and
suffering. In fact, the tragedy of
man is that so much of
our history is a history of
indifference, dominated by
a famous statement,
"Am I my brother's keeper?"

Abraham Joshua Heschel

He has filled the hungry with good things
but has sent the rich away empty.

Luke 1:53

W hen the disciples are confronted with a crowd of hungry people, they tell Jesus to send the crowd into the surrounding villages so people can buy food. "You give them something to eat," Jesus says in response. And few of us would argue that later on, when Christ commissions Peter to feed his sheep, he's speaking only metaphorically. The church has been given the sacred responsibility of feeding, clothing, and sheltering those in dire need. Ours is a physical no less than spiritual gospel— good news meant for whole people, bodies and souls. Yet too many times the church celebrates God's provision without bringing that provision to bear on the most economically vulnerable. Too many times, the rich are filled with good things while the hungry are sent away empty.

A line forms down the sanctuary's center aisle. People stand in pairs at the front of the church, one holding the bread, another the cup. The bread has been broken. One by one, we who follow Jesus step forward to receive the sacraments. This is Christ's body, broken for you. Pieces of bread are dipped in the cup; they turn red. The blood of Christ, shed for you on the cross. Music is playing. Offerings are dropped in a basket. We are solemn and grateful. Once again, God's mercy has prevailed over sin. For another week, we are saved from ourselves. We are not forsaken. God has come to us in our great need. We taste and chew and swallow the grace of God. We say amen. We say thank you under our breath.

Meanwhile, other lines form. On city sidewalks, people line up in front of shelters, food pantries, unemployment offices. They are like us—each a son or daughter of someone, each created, according to the Psalms, only a little lower than the angels. They collect in subway stations and under bridges and in public libraries during the day to sleep. In the last year, the number of those living on the streets in New York City has risen 34 percent. The homeless population has increased in every borough: by 228 people in Brooklyn, by 368 in Manhattan. City shelters are overwhelmed. The number of people in these shelters—38,000—is near the city's high. And New York is not unique. One in every 2,688 people in that city is homeless, compared with one in 1,810 in Chicago, and one in 154 in Los Angeles. These are our most recent and accurate figures.*

* Bosman, Julie. "Number of People Living on New York Streets Soars." The New York Times. March 19th, 2010.

At least two things must be said. First, when it comes to caring for the poor in our localities, the sheer magnitude of the task can tempt us to apathy. However, on this point the Scriptures are clear: neglect those among us who have material and physical needs, and our rituals are meaningless. Worse than meaningless—they make God sick. We must remember that the validity of our worship hinges on our commitment to the homeless and hungry outside our doors.

Second, many church leaders take this issue quite seriously. And each congregation has its own financial challenges, its own burdens to carry. But if God's provision is going to meet the poor where they live, we must honestly assess what our church budgets say about our true priorities. Is meeting the needs of the marginalized a central or peripheral concern? What material and aesthetic comforts are we addicted to, and what sacrifices must we make so that all people have their basic needs met? Is the gospel we preach good news for the rich and poor alike? Are both being filled?^

We need Christian communities who repeatedly ask such questions, and who arrange their economics in ways that humbly critique our culture for its excessive materialism. We need churches that commit to simplicity so that when they celebrate the goodness of God, the needy among them have reason to celebrate too.

^In his book *Just Generosity,* Ron Sider argues that if all Christians in North America tithed, the church could feed all the hungry and fund basic education for all the world's children plus have enough to fund the evangelistic ministries of the Church.

Questions
we must ask
One Another

Does the way our church handles finances give the poor reason to celebrate? Or are we in danger of engaging in meaningless rituals?

To what degree does the gospel we are proclaiming have an economic dimension?

What about our communal life together exhibits excess and waste? How might we need to deprive ourselves for the sake of others?

How does seeing human bodies as the temple of God change the way we think about a church building? About the Church's economics?

How can we begin to practically provide for each other as needs arise?

MATT. 6:11, LUKE 11:3

The book of Proverbs says, "Give me neither poverty nor riches. For in my poverty I could be forced to steal, or in my riches I could forget my God." And the vision that we see in Scripture is one where it"s neither people living in poverty nor in super affluence, but people who are living into this idea that we need this day our daily bread. Not for "me"…"my daily bread," but "our"… "…this day our daily bread." For all of us. And until that is fulfilled, we have to hunger for justice and for righteousness. We've got to hunger with the poor. We've got to fast from the luxuries of this world to make sure that other people can have their essentials.

PROVERBS 30:8-9, THE ENTIRE PASSAGE READS, "KEEP FALSEHOOD AND LIES FAR FROM ME; GIVE ME NEITHER POVERTY NOR RICHES, BUT GIVE ME ONLY MY DAILY BREAD. OTHERWISE, I MAY HAVE TOO MUCH AND DISOWN YOU AND SAY, 'WHO IS THE LORD?' OR I MAY BECOME POOR AND STEAL AND SO DISHONOR THE NAME OF MY GOD."

ACTS 5:1-11

In the early church, we catch this vision of the shared economics...was so critical. One of the first stories of the early church is actually kind of a terrible story. It"s the story of Ananias and Sapphira, who...as the offering is passing...they withhold from the common fund, and they lie about it to God. And you have this scene where God just strikes them dead. (I guess we should be kind of glad God"s not into that as much these days, or we"d have much smaller congregations.) But it really stresses how critical it was to this early church community that everybody share the things that they have, and they not lie about it, and that they not hold back from what God"s doing. That God"s doing a new thing. And that new thing means we"ve got to hold our possessions very lightly because when we cling to our own stuff, we enter back into the world of Pharaoh, where we"re stockpiling our stuff for tomorrow while other people don"t even have their bread today.

IT'S INTERESTING, AND SAD, THAT SO MANY OF GOD'S PEOPLE TODAY RESEMBLE THE EGYPTIANS WHO ENSLAVE AND STOCKPILE.

WHAT ARE YOU STOCKPILING FOR TOMORROW?

So the prophets really cry out that
our worship and our holy days and
feasts for God are detestable in
God"s sight if the poor aren"t cared
for. Amos cries out that we should
shut up with our singing and our worship if justice doesn"t roll out like
a mighty water to the poor...if there
isn"t justice for the poor, our in-
cense is stench in God"s nose and our
songs are noise in God"s ears; that
God cares about how our worship works
itself out for the most vulnerable
people in the land.

Amos 5: 11-13, 21-24; 8:4-10

Let's start to reimagine some of
these ancient and beautiful ideas because the patterns of the Gospel have
a whole lot to offer the world that we
live in right now.

Consider again these words:

"Give me neither poverty nor riches. For in my poverty I could be forced to steal, or in my riches I could forget my God." The Western drive to accumulate and consume contradicts this way of living. Are you willing to live another way?

To pray Proverbs 30:8-9 and see what happens?

What does it mean to hunger for justice and righteousness?

To hunger with the poor

Do y
state
and b
opinic
shape
words

Although biblically
sound, Relational
Tithe's way of living
may be completely
foreign to some of us.
What concrete changes
can we make so as to
begin to be reconciled
to the poor in our
communities?

principles?

ble
gn,
s no

Think of Matthew, the tax collector who responded to Jesus's call to "Follow me" by giving up his profession and literally following Christ (Matthew 9:9-13).

Now consider Zacchaeus, a tax collector who responded to Jesus by remaining in his profession but rectifying past wrongs (Luke 19:1-10).

Jesus rejoiced at both responses. How will you respond to Jesus's call to follow him and live in friendship with your community, loving your neighbor as yourself?

We helped others, it is true, but we did not deprive ourselves in order to help others. We had no philosophy of poverty.

Dorothy Day,
The Long Loneliness

When the righteous
prosper, the city rejoices;
when the wicked perish,
there are shouts of joy.

Proverbs 11:10

n the NIV, there's a heading over a passage in Acts Chapter 4 that reads, "The Believers Share Their Possessions," and it's a phrase in which we see belief and action joined together like a husband and wife. Which has me reflecting on this movement we call the church and on the dual importance of right thinking and right living. Both are present in communities that manifest God's kingdom. Both matter. Yet it seems that many of us have inherited a version of Christianity in which sound thinking (orthodoxy) invariably comes first. Meaning, we often feel the need to completely iron out our theology before we enact our theology. We feel the pressure to resolve all our questions about a given issue—an issue like shared economics, for instance—and to figure out exactly what we believe before we start behaving in new ways.

COMMENTARY

But what if the way to sound theology
is through our hands and feet? "Follow
me," Jesus tells his disciples, and it is
intriguing to notice that near the end of
their shared life on the road, the disciples
are still saying things like "Oh, now we
get it."** "Take up your mat and walk,"
Jesus tells the paralyzed man, and it's not
until the man stands up that he knows for
certain that Jesus has authority to heal
or to forgive sin. "Let down your nets
for a catch," Jesus says to Peter, and it is
when Peter does what Jesus says that the
truth about God's extravagance brings
him to his knees. Those who follow
Jesus with their hands, their feet, their
resources, their wills, find themselves
thinking in ways they wouldn't have
thought otherwise. The beauty of Christ's
teachings—orthodoxy itself—opens up to
them from the inside.

** John 16:30: "Now we can see that you know all things
and that you do not even need to have anyone ask you
questions. This makes us believe that you came from God."
Jesus's response (v. 31): "You believe at last!"

This reality applies not only to the lives of individual Christ followers but to our collective life also. To borrow an image from the theologian Karl Barth[^^], reading biblical accounts of the early church is like standing at a window and seeing a crowd in the street. The people are looking up at the sky, pointing at something. They seem excited. We try to get a glimpse of what they're pointing at, but our view is blocked by the overhanging roof. We cannot see the vision from where we're standing. We can't comprehend it. And when it comes to enacting a new and compassionate economy, the early church pushes us to leave our place at the window—to move beyond spectatorship, beyond conversations about the church, and to begin looking for concrete ways to share what we have, just to see what happens. Those first Christians challenge us to experiment with patterns of relating to each other that are wildly unfamiliar and to let our *thinking* about community be transformed by our *practice*.

^^ From *The Word of God and the Word of Man*. Frederick Buechner borrowed the image from Barth. I borrowed from Buechner.

Granted, for many of us this will mean becoming less financially secure. We may have to dismantle the material scaffolding we've erected around our lives, casting off possessions for the sake of others, as many people much poorer than we have done since this movement began. For some of us, this will mean getting over ourselves enough to allow our community to provide for us—confessing our material needs and having the humility to receive help. For all of us, this will mean a fiercer commitment to one another, a fiercer loyalty, as each of us considers everyone else more important than ourselves.

Are we willing to live this way? Are we at least willing to try? In a cultural moment in which our fragile national economy is a source of great anxiety and fear, the Scriptures point to such concrete expressions of love as fear's antidote. With this truth in mind, may we who make up the church of Jesus try to arrange our daily economics in a way that God's love for all people is consistently felt. And may our hands and feet lead us to places we would otherwise not go.

Questions
we must ask **One Another**

When considering the idea of shared economics,
what questions arise?

What thoughts or feelings prevent you from
experimenting with this way of living?

*Have you had any experience with
relational redistribution? How did that
experience change the way you think
about stuff?*

What about being openhanded with your possessions
makes you uncomfortable? Which of
your possessions do you feel most attached to or
most territorial about?

Are you willing to fast from certain luxuries, to practice simplicity, so that others might receive their daily bread? Which luxuries?

Will you let your hands and feet lead you into a new understanding of Christian community?

If so, how will you begin?

THE STORY OF
RELATIONAL TITHE

RELATIONAL TITHE: FROM PHILANTHROPY TO FRIENDSHIP

Relational Tithe, founded by Darin Petersen and Shane Claiborne, exists to live out the hope that we can create a network of relationships to share financial resources and burdens. It encourages us to think of those in need in ways that promote us to live well and in solidarity with our local and global neighbors. Since economic and relational poverty are both realities, we believe that alternative economic structures are needed within our world to ensure that the poor among us are cared for.

Possibly what most makes Relational Tithe unique is that *value is found less in the tithe and more in the relationship.* We are not an organization offering services as much as a community offering community and friendship. Within the context of friendship and a common commitment to overcome barriers that tend to keep us isolated from our neighbor, we share a tenth of our income for need-meeting.

Instead of simply brokering resources through macro-charity, both the giver and receiver are relationally connected, facilitating the reallocation of resources in a way that seeks to dismantle inequality through intimate sharing. To that end, individuals contribute a portion of their financial resources and combine it with of a handful of others' resources; they commit to surfacing and bringing the needs of their neighbors, family, and friends before the group to present and discuss the opportunity for the group to meet the needs of those with whom they are in relationship.

The power of this shared responsibility has been staggering. In a short period of time, one small group of redistribution provided sustainable job creation in Philadelphia, basic food needs in the Caribbean, transportation for a single parent in California, housing in Cairo, microenterprise development in Nigeria, agricultural initiatives in Ghana and the Caribbean, health care in North Carolina, and a proper funeral for a thirteen-year-old Sudanese refugee in Nebraska. The stories, lives, and friendships that those stories represent are endless and ongoing.

It is our desire to make resource reallocation more accessible to both those who have much and those who have little. Just as many hands make for light work, many friends make burdens, including financial burdens, lighter.

KEY IDEAS

This described reality, formed by Relational Tithe's founders, remains the guiding force for expanding partnerships and distinguishes Relational Tithe from other groups and communities seeking to do God's work in the world in their own valuable ways. The uniqueness of Relational Tithe is found in the following underlying and ever-present values.

ECONOMY OF ENOUGH

Relational Distribution (Tithe) is rooted in an idea that is both new and ancient—the economy of "enough." This is a different sort of economy, in which personal enrichment takes a backseat to the needs of the community. The problem is not that God created too many people and not enough stuff. The challenge is that we realize that there is enough for all of our needs, but there is not enough for all of our greed. Within Relational Tithe, one hundred percent of the tithe goes directly to meeting needs (not overhead or operational expenses) of those with whom we are relationally connected.

Relational Tithe allows us to effectively and collectively do what we are not able to do individually—namely to build genuine relationships that cross class boundaries, thereby making redistribution possible and personal. These connections, which span geographic and socioeconomic barriers, are at the heart of the Relational Tithe vision. Each recipient is in direct relationship with one of the participants of a Relational Tithe group. We see one degree of separation as a guide to insure that relationships—rather than simply sharing monies—are held to the utmost importance.

IMPARTIAL & EQUAL VOICE

In a world in which the one who holds the gold also makes the rules, we seek to remove the power of money and the illusion of security by refocusing the interaction around relationships. No matter the size of each participant's tithe, each voice is equal in the process of discussing, sharing and deciding how best to meet needs brought before a particular group.

TRANSPARENCY

Relational Distribution (Tithe) urges everyone to live financially transparent with their community of faith or wherever they are being nurtured spiritually. In the United

States, where personal financial transparency is near nonexistent, you dare not ask even the closest of friends how much money they make at the risk of getting a bodily response. We encourage one another to embrace distributional justice and live on ninety percent or less of our income. We believe we (individuals) are to live with the remaining personal income spread between meeting the needs of our nuclear family (personal housing, food, clothing, and so on) and the needs of our extended family (worship building, pastoral leaders, and so on). The idea of relational redistribution is an exercise in trust. I trust that the very group of which I'm a part will see the moments when I am without. If I see myself with a comparative abundance, I trust the collective wisdom of the group to help me share so that no one goes without.

THE TITHE AS A TOOL

With the desire to see the Church as a place where the collective sharing of resources is used to care for those on the margins (feed the hungry, clothe the naked, shelter the homeless, heal the sick, and visit the imprisoned), we see the tithe as a way to ensure no one goes without. When roughly only $5 of every $100 given to a congregation in the United States is given away and roughly only 2% of the annual income of the average congregant is shared, something seems contrary to the way Jesus modeled for us to care for one another. We believe relationships are an important part of giving. Rather than being detached from where our money/tithe/giving goes, relational redistribution (tithing) focuses us back on giving as an act of relationship building.

THE COVENANT OF THE CHARTER COMMUNITY

The Charter Community of Relational Tithe (the group stemming from the original Relational Tithe participants) collectively shares these values and, like each Relational Tithe group, chooses self-imposed requirements and goals in the form of a shared covenant.

This covenant describes their relational tithe not as independently operating individuals, but as a unified community participating together in the work of God in the world and the redistribution of God's abundant kingdom:

Because I share the hope of a relational transformation in myself and my community, and because I desire a collective sharing of resources in the church to feed the hungry, clothe the naked, shelter the homeless, heal the sick, and visit the imprisoned, 1) I commit 10 percent (a tithe) of my financial resources to the community of Relational Tithe for 6 months through the common fund. 2) I commit to honestly sharing the needs of my community and freely giving to other communities in need. My commitment to Relational Tithe is an effort to create personal relationships with others across lines of class, race and geography. It is an attempt to participate in the needs of the larger human community in a more intimate and financial way. 3) I commit to reconciliation through relationships, and I believe Relational Tithe provides this opportunity in a seamless platform of redistribution. 4) I commit to sharing myself in meeting the needs of those brought before the community by other covenant members of Relational Tithe. 5) I commit to participate in this need-meeting by actively making myself informed of the needs brought before Relational Tithe, and 6) am committed to sharing questions, ideas, and blessings to best collectively decide how to meet the need. 7) I commit to being transparent with my finances. I invite all other members of Relational Tithe to encourage and stretch my understanding and practice of biblical economics, and my life as a red-letter consumer.

UNDERSTANDING RELATIONAL TITHE ON THE WEB

With the separation of miles and oceans between participants, even within the same small groups of restitution, this project's sharing of needs and collective discussions of ways to meet them operates primarily in an online environment. We seek to develop an advanced and widely accessible software application that facilitates a seamless platform for economic and life sharing.

RelationalTithe.com is an interactive platform for connecting and meeting needs across socioeconomic and geographic barriers. It is also a place to explore, meet, share dreams and ideas, ask and discuss questions, and learn and grow together. We are determined to live intentionally, in joyful and responsible relationships with those around us. This site is only one, albeit powerful, tool to connect with people all over the world who share this vision.

THE TOOLS OF RELATIONAL TITHE MEMBER SERVICES

The goal of Relational Tithe Member Services is to help people and groups think about, talk about, and do relational redistribution in ways that give witness to an economy of abundance. If you're seeking to learn more about relational redistribution and are interested in helpful resources and assistance, Relational Tithe can help you. Participation with Relational Tithe Member Services is purely optional, but many have found it helpful in navigating the tools and process used by Relational Tithe for collective redistribution.

Whether you're looking for someone to conduct a workshop,

present a keynote address, or teach at your faith community gathering, Relational Tithe Member Services can be available to **speak** about our specific approach to relationships, money, poverty, and community. Maybe you, or a handful of you, are looking to start your own group and you are seeking to develop strategies for implementing a relational redistribution philosophy; Member Services can **consult. Coaching** is available to those who have started a group and are looking for ongoing encouragement and ways to connect with other like-minded groups. Or, maybe you wonder if you're ready to start a group or are looking to strengthen your existing commitment as a people; Member Services can walk with you to **assess** your areas of strength along with areas needing development. The logistics of a group's activity, from contributions to sharing actual resources with a recipient, can be quite daunting for an individual or small group of people, so Relational Tithe Member Services has provided a way for your group to focus on relational redistribution while they provide this oversight and **management** services to you. As the name suggests, Member Services is simply a mechanism by which to encourage, empower, and support members of Relational Tithe.

INQUIRIES FOR RELATIONAL TITHE

Email: memberservices@relationaltithe.com
Web: RelationalTithe.com

NOTES

JOURNEY THROUGH ECONOMY OF LOVE WITH YOUR COMMUNITY:

ECONOMY OF LOVE: SMALL GROUP EDITION
Creating a Community of Enough

A Resource of Relational Tithe

Includes 5 Video Sessions with Shane Claiborne

To order go to thehousestudio.com or economyoflove.org

OTHER RESOURCES FROM THE HOUSE STUDIO:

NEW!

the sinai experiment
Ten Words for God's Chosen People
Ryan Scott

The Sinai Experiment
Ten Words for God's Chosen People

thehousestudio.com